Pat, Pat, Pat!

By Cameron Macintosh

I am Tam.

I pat Mats.

Sam and Pip sit.

Sam pats Pip.

Pat, pat, pat!

It is Tim.

Tim pats Mat and Mip.

Pat, pat, pat!

Pam pats Mim.

Mim pats Pam!

Pat, pat, pat!

CHECKING FOR MEANING

1. Who pats Pip? *(Literal)*

2. Who pats Pam? *(Literal)*

3. Do you think Mim liked being patted? *(Inferential)*

EXTENDING VOCABULARY

am	What are the sounds in *am*? Which letter is added to the front of *am* to make *Tam*?
sit	Look at the word *sit*. What smaller word from the book is at the end of *sit*? What other words do you know that end with this word?
pat	Look at the word *pat*. What other things might you pat besides a pet?

MOVING BEYOND THE TEXT

1. Which pets from the book did you like best? Why?

2. What do you need to do to care for a dog that you don't need to do for a cat or chicken?

3. What is your ideal pet? Why?

4. What are some places that you might take pets to?

SPEED SOUNDS

Mm	Ss	Aa	Pp	Ii	Tt

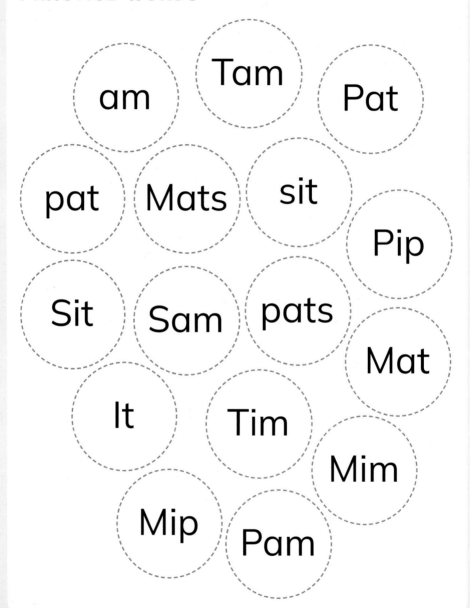

am

Tam

Pat

pat

Mats

sit

Pip

Sit

Sam

pats

Mat

It

Tim

Mim

Mip

Pam